Andrew

Story written by Gill Munton
Illustrated by Tim Archbold

Speed Sounds

Consonants *Ask children to say the sounds.*

f ff (ph)	l ll (le)	m mm mb	n nn (kn) gn	r rr wr	s ss se c ce	v ve	z zz se s	sh	th	ng nk

b bb	c k ck	d dd	g gg gu	h	j g ge	p pp	qu	t tt	w (wh)	x	y	ch tch

Each box contains one sound but sometimes more than one grapheme.
*Focus graphemes for this story are **circled**.*

Vowels

Ask children to say the sounds in and out of order.

a	e	i	o	u	ay	ee	igh	ow
	ea				a͡-e	ea	i͡-e	o͡-e
					a	e	ie	oa
					ai	y	i	o
					aigh		y	oe

oo u͡-e ue ew	oo	ar	or	air	ir	ou	oy	ire	ear
			oor	are	ur	ow	oi		
			ore		er				
			aw						

Story Green Words

Ask children to read the words first in Fred Talk and then say the word.

view   shore   phew   crew   threw   newt   deck   stew   eye*

Ask children to say the syllables and then read the whole word.

Tues|day   Stew|art   news|pap|er   a|muse   life|boat   wet|suit*

Ask children to read the root first and then the whole word with the suffix.

dune → dunes   bob → bobbed   listen → listening

confuse → confused   rescue → rescued   brew → brewed

unscrew → unscrewed   gentle → gently

* Challenge Words

Vocabulary Check

Discuss the meaning (as used in the story) after the children have read each word.

	definition:	sentence:
cool bag	a bag that keeps food cold	We took a picnic in a cool bag …
sand dunes	small sandy hills by the sea	… and sat on the sand dunes.
bobbed	moved	My boat bobbed gently up and down.
confused	in a muddle	When I woke up, I felt confused. Where was I?
shore	the beach	I knew I was too far from shore.
crew	people who work on the boat	One of the crew threw me a lifebelt.
deck	outside walking area on a boat	He carried me up a ladder to the deck.

Red Words

great	brother	above	where
could	was	what	here
someone	through	another	there
school	water	of	were
to	all	one	want

Andrew

Tuesday June 28th

The first day of the school holidays.
I went to the beach with my big brother Stewart.

It was a day I knew I'd never forget.
A day when I was a fool.

We took a picnic in a cool bag and sat on the sand dunes.
We had a great view of the smooth blue sea,
and we were both in a good mood.

Stewart started to read his newspaper, and left me to amuse myself.
I took my new blow-up boat down to the sea.

I lay in my boat, listening to the sound of the waves.
A few noisy seagulls flew above my head, swooping to catch fish.
My boat bobbed gently up and down, up and down ...

When I woke up, I felt confused.
Where was I?

The wind blew much harder now...
The waves grew bigger, and bigger,
all the time ...

Water slopped into my little boat, and my legs felt wet and cold.

I looked for Stewart, but I could only just see the beach.
I knew I was too far from shore.

I was really scared now.

What if my boat sank?

Or what if I floated here for ever?

Then someone shouted, "Andrew! Andrew! Can you see me?"

A motorboat – red, white and blue –
was bumping through the huge waves.

It drew closer.

It hooted its horn.

It was a lifeboat!

Phew! I was going to be rescued, at last.

One of the crew threw me a lifebelt
and told me to put it on.

Another man jumped into the water
and swam out to me.
He looked like a newt in his black wetsuit.
He pulled me to the lifeboat
and carried me up a ladder to the deck.

We were soon back on shore.
Mum and Dad were there – and Stewart.
Mum had given him a good telling off
for not looking after me.

The lifeboat crew had brewed up some hot tea.
Dad unscrewed the flask and filled a mug for me.

Later, safe at home, Mum gave me some hot stew. As I chewed the meat, I was thinking how stupid I'd been. I couldn't put all the blame on Stewart.

I was thinking that we both needed a set of rules,
to keep us safe in the water.

Rules for swimming in the sea

1 Don't swim straight after eating.

2 Don't swim alone. Don't let children out of your sight.

3 Don't use blow-up toys on a windy day.

4 Get out of the water if you feel too cold.

5 Keep an eye on the tide.

6 Look out for red flags. They mean "No swimming".

Questions to talk about

Ask children to TTYP each question using 'Fastest finger' (FF) or 'Have a think' (HaT).

p.9   (FF)   Where did Andrew and Stewart sit to have their picnic?

p.10   (FF)   What did Andrew do while his brother was reading?

p.11   (FF)   How did Andrew know that he was too far from the shore?

p.12   (FF)   What did Andrew see coming closer?

p.13   (HaT)   Why did the man look like a newt?

p.14   (FF)   Why did they both need a set of rules?

p.15   (HaT)   Which do you think is the most important rule?

Questions to read and answer

(Children complete without your help.)

1. What did Andrew and Stewart take to the beach?

2. What had happened to Andrew while he was asleep?

3. Who saved Andrew?

4. Why was Stewart told off?

5. Why did Andrew write a set of rules for swimming in the sea?

Speedy Green Words

knew	forget	blue	boat
white	rules	safe	mean
first	listening	little	when
good	started	catch	time
really	red	out	looked